T0418305

POODLES

BY LIBBY WILSON

Copyright © 2025 by Apex Editions, Mendota Heights, MN 55120. All rights reserved. No part of this book may be reproduced or utilized in any form or by any means without written permission from the publisher.

Apex is distributed by North Star Editions:
sales@northstareditions.com | 888-417-0195

Produced for Apex by Red Line Editorial.

Photographs ©: Shutterstock Images, cover, 1, 6, 7, 9, 10–11, 12–13, 14, 15, 16–17, 18, 19, 20–21, 22–23, 24, 25, 29; Stephen Smith/Sipa USA/AP Images, 4–5; iStockphoto, 26–27

Library of Congress Control Number: 2023922212

ISBN
978-1-63738-912-6 (hardcover)
978-1-63738-952-2 (paperback)
979-8-89250-049-4 (ebook pdf)
979-8-89250-010-4 (hosted ebook)

Printed in the United States of America
Mankato, MN
082024

NOTE TO PARENTS AND EDUCATORS

Apex books are designed to build literacy skills in striving readers. Exciting, high-interest content attracts and holds readers' attention. The text is carefully leveled to allow students to achieve success quickly. Additional features, such as bolded glossary words for difficult terms, help build comprehension.

TABLE OF CONTENTS

CHAPTER 1

SHOW DOG

A large poodle lies on a grooming table. Her name is Siba. Siba's handler prepares her for a show. The handler cleans and styles Siba's hair.

Handlers brush and blow-dry parts of a poodle's hair. Other parts are shaved.

FAST FACT

Show poodles often have large puffs of hair. These can take hours to style.

Handlers can use bands to style a poodle's hair.

Siba competed in the Westminster Kennel Club Dog Show. This show is one of the oldest and most famous in the world.

Later, Siba and her handler enter the show ring. The crowd cheers. Siba poses for them. Then she trots around the ring.

A judge studies Siba's body and **gait**. Siba is named Best in Show. This is the top award. Siba gets a treat to celebrate.

JUDGING

Judges compare each dog to its **breed** standard. This list tells how a dog breed should look and move. Judges decide which dog matches its standard best. This dog wins.

Siba beat more than 2,600 other dogs to win Best in Show.

CHAPTER 2

ALL-PURPOSE DOGS

The poodle breed began 400 years ago in Germany. The dogs swam to **retrieve** ducks shot by hunters. Their name came from the German word *pudelin*. It means "to splash."

Many poodles love being in the water.

Poodles often have puffs on their hips, chests, and ankles. The fur keeps those body parts warm.

Early poodles were working dogs. But by the 1700s, poodles became popular with French lords and ladies. People gave these dogs fancy hairdos.

HELPFUL HAIRCUTS

Working poodles often retrieved birds in icy water. Their thick hair kept them warm. But it dragged them down. So, owners shaved parts of the dog's coats. They left other parts long.

By the 1900s, many people had smaller poodles. The dogs were easier to take care of.

People also began breeding smaller poodles. These dogs became popular pets in many countries. People also trained poodles for jobs. Many poodles worked as service dogs.

FAST FACT

Some poodles became circus dogs. They were **athletic** and learned tricks quickly.

People can train circus poodles to dance or jump through hoops.

CHAPTER 3

POODLE TRAITS

Today, poodles come in three sizes. Standard poodles are the largest. They weigh 40 to 70 pounds (18 to 32 kg).

Standard poodles are at least 15 inches (38 cm) tall at the shoulder.

Miniature poodles are between 10 and 15 inches (25 and 38 cm) tall at the shoulder.

Miniature poodles weigh 10 to 15 pounds (5 to 7 kg). Toy poodles are the smallest. They weigh 4 to 6 pounds (2 to 3 kg).

FAST FACT

People began breeding toy poodles in the early 1900s. They wanted small dogs that could live in apartments.

Toy poodles grow up to 10 inches (25 cm) tall at the shoulder.

All poodles have thick, curly coats. Their hair comes in many colors. Most often, it is white, black, or brown.

ALLERGIES

Many people are **allergic** to dog hair. But a poodle's hair sheds very little. That makes poodles easier to be around for people with allergies.

Poodles are usually solid-colored. But some have two or more colors.

CHAPTER 4

POODLE CARE

All poodles are active dogs. They need one to two hours of exercise every day. Owners can take poodles on walks.

Even small poodles need daily exercise.

Poodles may chew or rip things if left alone too long.

Poodles also need lots of time with their owners. Poodles may get **anxious** if left alone too long. Instead, owners should train them and play with them.

POODLE PERSONALITY

Poodles have playful and silly **personalities**. Yet they are also **elegant**. Poodles are one of the smartest dog breeds. They want to please their owners.

Poodles can learn many different tricks.

Many owners pay groomers to trim and clean their dogs' hair.

Poodle hair requires a lot of care. It must be clipped every four to six weeks. Owners should also brush their dogs daily.

FAST FACT

Some poodles get sporting cuts. In this style, the dog's hair is short all over.

COMPREHENSION QUESTIONS

Write your answers on a separate piece of paper.

1. Write a few sentences explaining the main ideas of Chapter 2.

2. If you were getting a poodle, which size would you choose? Why?

3. What country are poodles from originally?

    A. France

    B. Germany

    C. the United States

4. Why would small dogs work well in apartments?

    A. Small dogs need to eat a lot.

    B. Small dogs shed more often.

    C. Small dogs don't need much space.

5. What does **trots** mean in this book?

*Siba poses for them. Then she **trots** around the ring.*

    A. holds still

    B. drinks water

    C. jogs

6. What does **active** mean in this book?

*All poodles are **active** dogs. They need one to two hours of exercise every day.*

    A. needing to move around

    B. needing to take naps

    C. needing to go home

Answer key on page 32.

GLOSSARY

allergic
Reacting to something by feeling sick.

anxious
Afraid or worried.

athletic
Showing speed, strength, or other active skills.

breed
A specific type of dog that has its own looks and abilities.

elegant
Very graceful and grand.

gait
The way an animal walks.

personalities
The ways that people or animals usually act.

retrieve
To go get something and bring it back.

BOOKS

Adelman, Beth. *Poodles*. Minneapolis: Kaleidoscope, 2020.

Noll, Elizabeth. *Toy Dogs*. Minneapolis: Bellwether Media, 2021.

Pearson, Marie. *Dogs*. Mankato, MN: The Child's World, 2020.

ONLINE RESOURCES

Visit **www.apexeditions.com** to find links and resources related to this title.

ABOUT THE AUTHOR

Libby Wilson has loved books and reading her entire life. She enjoys researching and finding interesting facts to share with readers. Her favorite topics are nature, history, and inspirational people. For the past 11 years, Ms. Wilson has been owned by Molly, the world's sweetest golden retriever.

INDEX

ANSWER KEY:
1. Answers will vary; 2. Answers will vary; 3. B; 4. C; 5. C; 6. A